Lost Boys of Sudan

John DiConsiglio

SCHOLASTIC INC.
New York Toronto London Auckland Sydney
Mexico City New Delhi Hong Kong Buenos Aires

Cover photo
© Hudson Derek/Corbis Sygma

Copyright © 2004 by Scholastic Inc.
All rights reserved. Published by Scholastic Inc.
Printed in the U.S.A.

ISBN 0-439-68252-5

2   3   4   5   6   7   8   9   10   23   12 11 10 09 08 07 06 05

Contents

Introduction

It was a quiet night in the south of Sudan, a country in Africa. Members of a tribe called the Dinkas were sleeping in their mud-walled huts. At a river nearby, boys from the tribe were **tending** cattle.

That's when soldiers from the north attacked.

Bullets blasted through the huts, shredding the grass roofs. The boys at the

tending taking care of something

river heard the shooting. They left their cattle and raced home, only to find their homes in flames and their families killed.

Afraid for their lives, the boys ran into the woods.

Soldiers had attacked other villages in southern Sudan, too. There were thousands of children hiding in the woods. Most were boys. Some were girls. None were older than 19. Many were as young as two. They were all **orphans**.

And they all knew they had to leave their country.

Sudan was in the middle of a terrible **civil war**. In a civil war, groups of people from the same country fight each other.

In Sudan, a government in the north ruled the whole country. But the Dinka

orphans children whose parents have died
civil war a war between different groups of people within the same country

and other people in the south had demanded their independence. That had led to civil war.

The 17,000 boys—and about 100 girls—who fled Sudan are called the Lost Boys. They walked more than 1,000 miles, through deserts, rivers, and battlefields. Many were killed by wild animals, disease, and **starvation**. Others made it to Ethiopia and Kenya.

You are about to meet three of these young people. They were separated from their families and their country. They narrowly escaped death. And along with over 4,000 other kids from Sudan, they started new lives in the United States.

In their own words, they tell a terrifying story of hope and survival.

starvation suffering and dying from lack of food

The Lost Boys' Journey

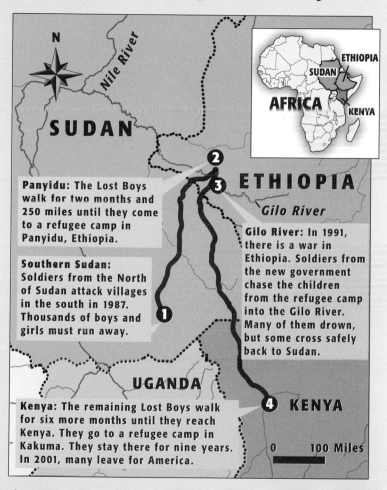

N

Nile River

SUDAN

ETHIOPIA

AFRICA

KENYA

ETHIOPIA

Panyidu: The Lost Boys walk for two months and 250 miles until they come to a refugee camp in Panyidu, Ethiopia.

Gilo River

Southern Sudan: Soldiers from the North of Sudan attack villages in the south in 1987. Thousands of boys and girls must run away.

Gilo River: In 1991, there is a war in Ethiopia. Soldiers from the new government chase the children from the refugee camp into the Gilo River. Many of them drown, but some cross safely back to Sudan.

UGANDA

❹ **KENYA**

Kenya: The remaining Lost Boys walk for six more months until they reach Kenya. They go to a refugee camp in Kakuma. They stay there for nine years. In 2001, many leave for America.

0   100 Miles

The Lost Boys walked north from southern Sudan to Ethiopia, and then south to Kenya. Those who survived walked about 1,000 miles.

Joe LeMonnier © Scholastic Inc

7

"Bullets don't care if you are a little girl. Everybody has to run for their lives."

1

Pia Mickliana Peter

My life stopped at 14. That's when the government soldiers destroyed my village. Before then, I was just a normal Sudanese girl from the Dinka tribe. I lived with my parents, my three sisters, and my three brothers in a small village called Chukudum.

Our village was surrounded by grass that grew eight feet high and by

Pia Mickliana Peter remembers, "In the 1980s, our peaceful lives changed. The northern government attacked us."

mountains that cast shadows across our fields.

Cattle were very important to us. We drank their milk. We used their skins for mats, clothes, and belts. Some kids in my village are even named after cattle.

In Dinka culture, the boys herd the cattle. Girls stay at home and work in the fields. At night, when the boys bring the cattle home from the river, the girls make the boys a stew of vegetables.

At 14, I was already engaged to a village boy. His name was John Omuno Derteo. I had known him since we were both little. Once, I made him a soccer ball out of banana skins. All the boys in my village kicked that ball. But John always made sure they let me play.

When our families arranged the marriage, his father gave us cattle as a gift for the right to marry me. That night we danced and sang in celebration. The Dinka love to sing.

But in the 1980s, our peaceful lives changed. The northern government attacked us. They bombed our countryside from planes. They raided towns and burned homes.

In 1987, the soldiers rolled into my village. It was **chaos**. There were bullets everywhere. And bullets don't care if you are a little girl. Everybody has to run for their lives.

In the madness, I grabbed my younger sisters and raced into the fields. For days, we hid in the grass. Shooting and

chaos terrible confusion

A soldier from the Sudan People's Liberation Army (SPLA) stands in a village in southern Sudan in 1991. The SPLA fought the government.

screaming filled the air. Bombs exploded around us. I held my sisters close.

I didn't know what happened to my parents or my brothers or John. But my little sisters were counting on me to protect them. I was only 14, but now I had to be the grown-up.

Why did Pia feel that she had to be the grown-up?

*"We walked to Ethiopia.
It was a very hard walk."*

2

John Bol Atem

It was 1988. I think I was seven, but I am not sure. Even today, I don't know exactly how old I am.

I was living with my grandmother in a southern Sudanese village called Kongor. She and I were walking to our village one night when we heard planes over our heads. It was the government army attacking us. They wanted to kill

John Bol Atem says that during the walk, "We heard gunshots and fighting, and sometimes a hyena or a lion leaped from the grass."

us because we were from the Dinka tribe.

Bombs dropped everywhere. I ran with my grandmother. It was madness. Crowds of people fled their homes. Families called out to each other. Children cried for their mothers. In the darkness and confusion, I let go of my grandmother's hand. I never saw her again.

I was very young and scared. But boys from other villages helped me. They were only 13 or 14 years old. But we looked at them like grown-ups.

We walked to Ethiopia. It was a very hard walk. We walked through deserts and through forests of long grass. We ate berries off the trees and drank rain water. Many times, we were so thirsty, we had no choice but to drink our own urine.

Sometimes, we heard gunshots and fighting nearby. Sometimes, a hyena or a lion leaped from the grass. The animals took children and ran away. When we began our walk, there were many boys—thousands of boys. Many of them died along the way.

We walked for months until we came to Ethiopia. We stayed for three years. I made friends with six other boys. But then a war broke out in Ethiopia. We had to run again.

We ran back to the border of Sudan and Ethiopia. We came to a big river, called the Gilo River. It was raining and the water was rough. We had to jump in. Soldiers shot at us. Many children

Young people stand beneath a sign in the refugee camp of Kakuma, in Kenya. John Bol Atem was one of the 16,000 children in this camp.

drowned. But my friends and I made it to the other side.

We wandered for months before we came to Kenya in 1992. We lived in a crowded **refugee** camp in a city called Kakuma. We went to school. Doctors took care of us when we were sick. But there were no parents, no one who really watched after us.

I always thought I would go home again. But there was no home left for me in Sudan. When workers asked me and my friends what we wanted, we said we wanted to go to America.

refugee having to do with people who have been forced to leave their homes

3

Marko Aguer Ayii

I don't remember anything about my home country of Sudan—except leaving it. I was just two when the soldiers attacked. I don't remember my mother at all. A man carried me to safety when the shooting started. I don't know if he was a relative or a friend or a stranger.

I was six when I reached the refugee camp in Kakuma. I grew up in a refugee

Marko Aguer Ayii says, "A man carried me to safety when the shooting started. I don't know if he was a relative or a friend or a stranger."

camp. We played a little. We played soccer. But it was very hard. You don't get to be young. You have no childhood. You can play, but you are always afraid something will happen to you.

We had just a handful of grain to eat each day. Diseases spread through the camp, killing hundreds of people.

Still, we had schools where I studied math and English. And I made friends. Three older boys took care of me.

Then one day, people from the **United Nations** asked some of us if we wanted to go to the U.S. On July 17, 2001, I came to Atlanta, Georgia. I was 14.

Everything in America seemed strange to me. The buildings were so tall. The cars moved so fast. I had never seen a

United Nations a group of countries that tries to solve serious problems in the world

refrigerator or a stove—or even a toilet.

My **immigration** papers said I was 23. So, instead of going to school, I worked at a meat-packing plant. I worked from five in the morning to seven at night.

Then a woman from church asked me how old I was. When I told her I was just 14, she said I had to stop working and go to school.

Now I am 17, and I live with an American family. I go to high school. The school is very different from my school in Kakuma. In Kakuma, we wore uniforms. If we talked back, our teachers hit us.

My new school is hard. It's so big that I get lost going from class to class. The students talk fast and loud. But they are also very nice to me. They help me with

immigration having to do with moving from one country to live in a new country

my English. And they ask me about Africa. I don't know what to say. I could tell them the sad history of Sudan. But I would rather talk about Africa's green forest where you can eat mangos right off the trees, or how my Dinka tribe loves to sing in celebration.

I barely remember my country. But someday, when there is peace in Sudan, I will go back and help rebuild it. And that's the day when I will really sing.

Marko barely remembers Sudan. Why do you think he wants to go back?

*"I want to get an education.
I have so many dreams."*

Where Are They Now?

Pia, John, and Marko told incredible stories about their experiences in Sudan. So what happened to them next?

Pia Mickliana Peter

Pia hid in the mountains with her little sisters for a year, running from snakes, poisonous monkeys, and even elephants. But eventually, soldiers found them, and

Pia holds a picture of her fiance, John. She wants to return to her country and teach girls. In Sudan, she says, "there is not much schooling for girls. That is something I want to change."

Pia and her sisters were separated.

Pia joined some lost boys traveling to the Kakuma refugee camp. There, she met up with John, the young man she had been planning to marry.

In 2003, when Pia was 25, a church group helped her move to the U.S. She now lives near Denver, Colorado and works at a Target store. John hopes to join her.

After Pia moved to the U.S., she learned that her whole family had survived. Her parents and sisters are still living in Sudan. Her brothers are in Canada.

Pia hopes to go to school and become a teacher so she can return to Sudan and teach girls. "There will be a new Sudan someday," Pia says, and she wants to be part of it.

John Bol Atem, who in 2004 estimated that he was about 23, is going to college in Charlotte, North Carolina. He is studying law.

John Bol Atem

John Bol Atem and six of his friends came to the United States together in 2000. John settled in Charlotte, North Carolina. He got his high school diploma in May 2003. "It was the happiest day of my life," he says. He is currently attending community college in Charlotte and also works at a T.J. Maxx department store.

John left behind six brothers and one sister. One of his brothers was killed in the government raids. Another brother, who now lives in Uganda, told him that his grandmother was killed by soldiers too.

After college, John wants to study law. He isn't sure if he will ever go back to Sudan. "When I started my journey, I never thought I could be happy again," he says. "But here in America, I am happy. It is a miracle."

Marko Aguer Ayii

In 2003, Marko was 17. He was in ninth grade at a high school in Atlanta, Georgia. His English was getting better,

Marko stands with friends in Atlanta, Georgia. From left to right, there's Marko, Carolyn Geddes, Susan Gordon, Wilson Dut, and Peter Aciek. "I remember almost nothing about Sudan," Marko says.

and he was making friends. He had also made the soccer team.

Marko has a lot of hope for the future. "I want to get my education. Maybe I want to be a teacher," he says. "I have so many dreams."

Glossary

chaos *(noun)* terrible confusion

civil war *(noun)* a war between different groups of people within the same country

immigration *(adjective)* having to do with moving from one country to live in a new country

orphans *(noun)* children whose parents have died

refugee *(adjective)* having to do with people who have been forced to leave their homes

starvation *(noun)* suffering and dying from lack of food

tending *(verb)* taking care of something

United Nations *(noun)* a group of countries that tries to solve serious problems in the world